THE ETERNITY OF THE WORLD

Boethius of Dacia

Translated by: D.P. Curtin

Dalcassian Publishing Company

Copyright @ 2008 Dalcassian Publishing Company

All rights reserved. No part of this publication may be reproduced, distributed, or transmitted in any form or by any means, including photocopying, recording, or other electronic or mechanical methods, without the prior written permission of the publisher, except in the case of brief quotations embodied in critical reviews and certain other non-commercial uses permitted by copyright law. For permission request, write to Dalcassian Publishing Company at dalcassianpublishing at gmail.com

ISBN: 979-8-8692-8304-7 (Paperback)

Library of Congress Control Number:
Author: Curtin, D.P. (1985-)

Printed by Ingram Content Group, 1 Ingram Blvd, La Vergne, Tennessee

First printing edition 2008.

THE ETERNITY OF THE WORLD

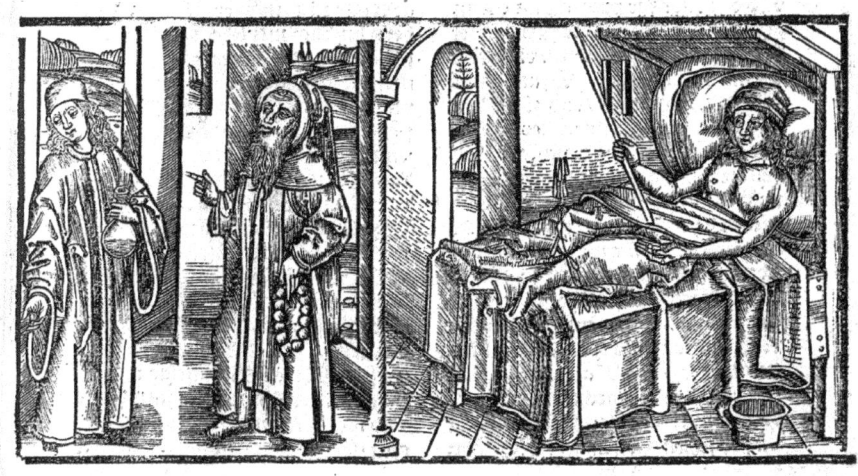

THE ETERNITY OF THE WORLD

1. Just as it is foolish to look for a reason in those things which must be believed according to the law, which have no reason for themselves, he who does this is looking for that which is impossible to find. And it is heretical not to believe them without reason, so in those things which they are not self-evident, which nevertheless have a reason for themselves, it is not philosophical to want to believe in them without reason. Therefore, wishing to bring the opinion of the Christian faith about the eternity of the world and the opinion of Aristotle and some other philosophers back into harmony, so that the opinion of the faith is firmly held even though in some that it cannot be demonstrated, lest we fall into folly, by seeking demonstration where it is not possible, lest we also fall into heresy, refusing to believe that which must be held by faith. Since it has no demonstration for itself, as was the custom of certain philosophers, to whom it pleased no law laid down, the articles the law laid down for them had no demonstration, so that even the opinion of the philosophers may be saved. As far as their reason can conclude, their opinion in nothing contradicts the Christian faith except among the unintelligent. For the opinion of the philosophers is based on demonstrations and certain possible reasons in the things of which they speak. Faith in many things rests on miracles and not on reasonings. For what is held because of what has been concluded by reason is

not faith but science, and so that it may be seen that faith and philosophy do not contradict themselves about the eternity of the world, so that it may also be clear that the reasons of certain heretics do not they have the strength by which, contrary to the Christian faith, they maintain that the world is eternal.

2. And it seems that it is not the case: the first principle is the cause of the substance of the world, because if it were not, then there would be more first principles. Yet, what has its existence from another, this follows that in duration. Therefore, the world follows the first principle in duration; but an eternal being has no sequel in duration. Therefore, the world is not eternal.

Likewise, nothing can be equal to God. If, therefore, the world was eternal, the world would be equal to God in duration; but this is impossible; therefore, et cetera.

Likewise, a finite power cannot make an infinite duration, because the duration does not exceed the making power itself; but the power of heaven is finite, just as the power of everybody is finite; therefore, the power of heaven does not make the duration eternal, therefore heaven is not eternal, therefore neither is the whole world, since the world does not precede heaven.

Likewise, God precedes the world according to nature, but in God nature and duration are the same; therefore, God precedes the world according to duration. Therefore, the world is not eternal.

Also, everything that is created is made from nothing: for in this, creation and generation differ, because all generation is from a subject and matter: therefore, the begetting cannot enter into the whole substance of a thing; but creation is not from the subject and matter, and therefore the creator can enter into the whole substance of the thing. Now the world was created, because before the world there was no subject and matter from which the world was made, therefore the world is from nothing. Since then, being and non-being could not be at the same time, therefore there was first non-being and afterwards being; but everything that has existence after non-existence is new; Therefore the world is new, therefore it is not eternal, since the new and the eternal do not sympathize in the same thing.

Again, to whom addition can be made, to that can be something greater; To all the time that preceded, time can be added, therefore also to all the time that preceded can be something greater. but nothing can be greater than infinity, therefore the whole time which has gone before is not infinite. Therefore, neither movement nor world.

Likewise, if the world were eternal, then the generation of animals and plants and simple bodies would be eternal; therefore, the individual would be shown from infinite generative causes: because if generation were eternal, then this individual man would be preceded by another, and that by another, and so ad infinitum. But it is impossible for one effect to be the result of an infinite number of active causes. First, therefore this generation is not eternal, therefore neither is the world.

Likewise, Aristotle says in Physics VI that magnitude, motion, and time are of the same reason, as far as finitude and infinity are concerned; therefore, since there is no magnitude infinite, as Aristotle proves in III Physics, therefore neither motion is infinite, nor time, therefore neither the world: since the world does not exist without these.

Likewise, if the world were eternal, then infinite men would be generated and corrupted, but in a corrupted man the substance that was in the body remains, the rational soul [of course], since it is itself ungenerative and incorruptible, and thus such substances would be infinite at the same time in action. but to be infinite [simultaneously] is actually impossible; therefore etc.

Likewise, if the world were eternal, then the motion would be infinite in transit and infinite time, because if the world were eternal, then the time preceding this instant would be infinite; but it is impossible for infinity to be traversed and received; therefore, etc.

Again, that which has another cause has this beginning; the world has another cause: therefore, the world has a beginning; "For the sea was made, because the world was made," as is said in II Meteors; that which has a beginning is not eternal; therefore, etc.

3. It is argued on the contrary, and first: that the world can be eternal, and that nothing follows from this is impossible; secondly, it is shown that the world is eternal. First thus: although the effect naturally follows its cause, yet it can be at the same time as its cause in duration; the world and all being is caused by the effect of the first being. Therefore, since the first being is eternal, the world can be eternal to itself. It is clear that the greater is because the priority and posteriority of nature and the simultaneity of duration are compatible with each other. It is also clear that the minor is because, just as in every genus it must first be the cause of all the others, so also in the genus of beings it must be that the first being is the cause of the others, and from this it follows that the first being must be an uncaused being, since it must itself be a sufficient cause. Of things, but nothing caused is a sufficient cause of any effect of its own, since on which the essence of a caused being depends, all its effect depends on the same; therefore the first being must be a being having no other cause: otherwise there would be no first being.

This same thing is seen by Aristotle in *Physics* VIII, who says that, although something is eternal, yet it must not be posited as a principle: for a triangle having three angles equal to two right angles is eternal, yet another cause of this eternal must be sought; therefore the eternal can have a cause; Since, therefore, nothing in duration can precede that which is eternal, therefore the effect can be coeternal with its cause. The world is the effect of the first being. Therefore, the world can be coeternal with itself.

Also, it is clear from the example: if the sun had always been in our hemisphere, light would always have been in the middle, and light would have been coeternal with the sun, and yet its effect, which would not be, unless the effect could be at the same time as its cause in duration.

Also, if the foot had always been in the dust, the footprint would have been coeternal with it, and yet its effect.

Likewise, this same argument is argued as follows: there is nothing eternal in the future without the past, because the power which can make the eternal duration of something in the future, can itself have made the eternal duration of the same thing in the past: since that power is unchangeable and always having itself in one way ; but the world is eternal in the future, and according to the opinion of the Christian faith, and according to the opinion of certain philosophers; therefore by the same virtue he could have been eternal in the past. Thus, then, the world can be eternal, and from this it seems that nothing impossible can be followed by reason, nor can anything objectionable be argued from this. And this will become clear to him who has set his heart on this.

4. Now that the world is eternal, it is argued thus:

> a. Everything that is incorruptible has the virtue of always being; because if he did not have such virtue, he would not be incorruptible. But the world is incorruptible, because everything that is born is incorruptible. Therefore, the world has power to be always; and a thing extends throughout the whole duration to which its power of being extends. Therefore, the world is eternal.

> b. Again, that is eternal which does not have any duration before it: for everything new has some duration before it; but the world had no duration before it, since it had no time: for there was no time before the world, because time follows the motion of the first mover, as the subject of passion. nor was there eternity before the world, since that which has eternal duration before it never exists. If, then, there had been eternal duration before the world, the world would never have been.

c. Likewise, what is done anew, this can be done, because if not, then what is impossible would be done; but by which a thing can be made, this is matter; but before the creation of the world there was no matter from which the world was made; therefore the world was not made anew, therefore it is eternal: since there is no middle ground between the new and the eternal.

d. Likewise, everything new is made by transmutation; since he who takes away the transformation takes away all newness; but every transformation has a subject and a matter, as it is written in the beginning of the 8th Metaphysics and the 7th of the same and the 3rd Physics: since motion and every change is an act of a being in power [and indeed] according to what is of this kind; since, therefore, before the world there was no matter and subject of transformation which would have been required for the new creation of the world, if the world had been a new fact; therefore the world is not a new creation, but eternal.

e. Also, everything is new in time, since it is new in some duration, it must be done in part of it: for what happens in a whole day is not new in a day, and what is in a whole year is not new in a year , but that which is new in a year must be in some part of the year, but among durations all only time has parts; Now the world naturally exists before time; therefore the world is not new, but eternal.

f. Also, every generation is from corruption, and everything corrupt was first generated; Similarly, all corruption is from what is generated, and everything that is generated is from what is corrupted. Therefore, before all generation is generation, and before all corruption is corruption. Therefore, it is not fitting to give the first generation nor the first corruption, therefore generation and corruption are eternal; therefore the world is eternal, because what is generated and decays are parts of the world which cannot precede the world in duration.

g. Again, the effect cannot follow its sufficient cause in duration. The sufficient cause of the world is eternal, because it is the first principle. Therefore, the world cannot follow it in duration; since the first principle is eternal, therefore the world is coeternal with itself. And the reason is confirmed: an eternal being, both according to its substance and according to all its disposition, to whom nothing is acquired in the future, and to whom nothing is lacking in the past from those by which it produced its effect, makes its immediate effect coeternal with itself; God is an eternal being according to substance and according to all that is in him, disposition, to whom nothing is acquired in the future, [and to whom] nothing is lacking in the past from those by which he produced his effect, and the world is his immediate effect; therefore the world is eternal to God.

h. Also, Aristotle says in *Metaphysics IX* that "the agent by will, when he can and wills, then acts, and it is not necessary to add, if he is not hindered: since being able removes the obstacle"; but God had from eternity the power and the will to make the world. Therefore, the world is an eternal fact.

i. Likewise, every new effect requires some novelty in some of its principles: since, if all the principles of an effect always had one way, the effect could not be made from them, since it did not exist before; but in the beginning of the world, which is the first being, no novelty is possible. Therefore, the world is not a new effect. And the reason is confirmed: if an agent is itself new according to its substance, it can itself be the cause of a new effect, either because it is itself eternal according to its substance, yet new according to some virtue or position - as appears in the body of heaven - or because it was previously subject to an impediment. or because a new arrangement has been made in the subject from which he acts; in the case of the world, none of these is possible, as it appears from itself. Therefore, the world is not caused to be new.

j. Likewise, everything that is moved after rest is reduced to a continuous motion that always is: since something that is sometimes moved, sometimes rests, could not happen from an immovable cause; since, therefore, he cannot proceed *ad infinitum* in motions, one of which is the cause of the other. Therefore, the first movement must be continuous and eternal. And for this reason, Aristotle, in *Physics VIII*, reduces every new motion to the first motion as to its cause, which, according to his opinion, is eternal; and Aristotle holds this opinion for this reason. A motion which always has sufficient causes cannot be new; but the first movement always has sufficient causes; because, if not, then another movement would have preceded it, by which it would have been sufficient in its causes, since it was not before, therefore it would be the first and not the first, which is impossible.

k. Again, the will which postpones the willed, expects something in the future. Before the world there is no expectation: because before the world there is no time, and there is no expectation except in time. Therefore, the world is not placed after the divine will, but that is eternal, therefore the world is co-eternal with the divine will.

l. Also, every effect which is sufficiently dependent on some will between which no duration falls between it and the will itself, is at the same time with that will: because they are together in duration, between which no duration falls, but the world is sufficiently dependent on the divine will, - another for it has no cause - and no duration falls between them, because there is no time; for before the world there was neither time nor eternity, because then there would be no world in eternity; therefore, since that which is in eternity is eternal, then if the world did not exist it would be eternal; therefore the world would never exist, which is impossible, therefore the world is co-eternal with the divine will.

m. Likewise, every new effect requires before it some transformation either in its agent, or in the subject from which it is produced, or at least that which is the arrival of the hour in which the agent, always having himself in one way, wants to act; before the world there could be no transformation. Therefore, the world cannot be a new effect.

5. Someone will answer that the world is indeed a new creation, because this was the form of the divine will from eternity, to produce the world at the hour in which it was made: for from the old will a new effect can proceed, and for this reason it is not necessary that any transformation should take place either in for someone now has the will to do something after three days, on the arrival of the third day he then does what he wanted before and from before, and yet there has not been any change in the will or in the willing. and in this way the world can be new, although it has an eternal [and] sufficient cause.

But it is argued against this way of putting it as follows: He who imagines what precedes, imagines everything that follows from it, and does not certify it. but you imagine in God such a form of the will from eternity, and you cannot make it clear, and thus it is easy to imagine everything: for someone will tell you that there was not such a form of the divine will from eternity, and you do not have it, wherefore you contradict him; therefore you also imagine that the world is new, and you will not be able to declare this.

Also, against the same mode of positing it is argued as follows: the will proceeds from the will according to the form of the will; If, then, the form of the divine will was such that it willed from eternity to produce the world in an hour, as you say, then it would have been impossible for God to have produced the world first, which seems inappropriate, since God is acting through the freedom of the will.

To this reason you will answer that, yes, God could have first made the world, because as he had this form of will from eternity, so he could have another, and therefore, just as he produced the world in the hour in which he was made, so he could have produced himself first.

But against this reason it is argued as follows: that which is of the will of one form and can be of another, this is transmutable according to wills; but God is completely unchangeable. Therefore, he cannot have another form of will than that which he had from eternity.

> n. Again, from the old will, between which the transmutation does not fall between it and its effect, no new effect can be made: for the effect is not at the same time as the cause in duration, this is done by the transmutation falling between them: for he who removes the transformation, himself removes all expectation; but no change can fall between the will of God, which is eternal, and the world; Therefore, before the world there can be no transformation; therefore the world is coeternal with the divine will.

> o. Also, according to the example that has been set, it is not appropriate in the purpose; namely, that a man now has the will to do something after three days, but on the arrival of the third day he does what he had wanted from before, that example is inappropriate in the purpose: because, although there has been no change in the will, nor in the willing, yet a change has been made which is the coming hour, that is, the third day. But if the transformation had not taken place in the willing, nor in the passive, from which the new effect should have been produced; nor could that transformation which is the coming of the hour, then by some will a new effect be made, because every new effect requires before it some transformation, as some might say. And since before the world there was no change in the will from which the world was made, nor in the matter from which the world should be made - since matter does not precede the world - nor was that change made before the world, which is the coming of some hour, then it seems that from the will the new world could not become eternal. And therefore, that example is inappropriate in purpose.

These are the reasons by which some heretics, who hold to the eternity of the world, endeavor to attack the opinion of the Christian faith, which posits that the world is new; against which it is expedient that a Christian should study diligently, so that he may know how to solve them perfectly, if any heretic opposes them. These are the reasons:

The solution

6. First, it must be carefully considered here that there is no question [that can be] debatable by reasons, which the philosopher should not discuss and determine, how the truth is in it, as far as it can be understood by human reason. And the explanation of this is that all the reasons by which it is argued are accepted from things: for otherwise they would be a figment of the understanding; But the philosopher teaches the natures of all things: for just as philosophy teaches being, so the parts of philosophy teach the parts of being, as is written in Metaphysics 4, and it is self-evident. Therefore, the philosopher has to determine every question that can be debated by reason: for every question that can be debated by reason falls into some part of being, but the philosopher contemplates every being: natural, mathematical, and divine. Therefore, the philosopher has to determine every disputable question by reason and let those who say the contrary know that he is ignorant of his own discourse.

Secondly, it must be noted that neither the naturalist, nor the mathematician, nor the metaphysician can show by reason that the first movement and the new world are.

7. But the fact that a naturalist cannot show this is made clear by accepting two suppositions known by themselves, the first of which is: that no artist can cause, grant, or deny anything except from the principles of his knowledge. The second assumption is that, although nature is not the first principle simply, it is nevertheless the first principle in the genus of natural things, and the first principle that can be considered natural. And therefore Aristotle, considering this in the book of Physics, which is the first book of natural doctrine, began not from the first principle simply, but from the first principle of natural things, that is, from the first matter, which in II of the same he says is nature. And from these to the purpose.

Nature cannot cause any new movement unless it is preceded by another movement which is its cause; but the first movement cannot be preceded by another movement, because then it would not be the first movement. Therefore, the naturalist, whose first principle is nature, cannot, according to his own principles, maintain that the first movement is new. The greater is clear, because material nature does nothing new unless it is first acted upon by another: for material nature cannot be the first mover. For how can a being begotten be the first mover? And every material agent is a begotten being. Nor is there an instance of the body of heaven, because if it is a material being, yet it does not have matter unequivocally with generable things; for they are transmutable to each other which share the matter of one nature.

Likewise, every new natural effect requires some novelty in its immediate principles; but novelty cannot exist in any being without a preceding transformation: for he who takes away the transformation, himself takes away the newness; Therefore, nature can cause no new motion or effect without a previous transformation. Therefore, according to nature, whose first principle is nature, the first movement, which no change can precede, cannot be new. The greater is evident, because if all the immediate principles of any natural effect had always been in the same arrangement, from them that effect could not be now, when it was not before. For I will ask why now more than before, and you have no way to answer. Now I say, in this respect, "immediate principles," because, although the natural effect is new, it is not necessary for this reason that there should be any change and novelty in its mediate and first principles. For although the proximate principles of generable things are changed, and sometimes they are, and sometimes they are not, yet they are always their first causes.

From these it is evident that the natural cannot posit any new movement, unless it is preceded by some movement which is the cause of it; therefore, since it is necessary to posit some first motion in the world - for it is not possible to go on ad infinitum in motions of which one is the cause of another - it follows that the natural man, from his knowledge and his principles which he uses, cannot posit a new first motion.

That is why Aristotle, in *Physics VIII*, asking whether motion was once made when it was not before, and using these principles which have just been stated, and speaking as if natural, posits the first eternal motion on both sides. He himself also in the same *Physics VIII*, asking why certain things sometimes move and sometimes remain at rest, answers that this is because they are moved by a mover who is always in motion. Because the motor by which they are moved is the motor of motion, it therefore behaves in different ways, and for this reason it causes its movable objects to sometimes move and sometimes to rest. But those things which are always in motion, such as the bodies of the heavens, are moved by an immovable mover, always having one way in themselves and in their movables.

If, therefore, the naturalist cannot, according to his own principles, posit the first new motion, then neither can the mobile [first] itself, because the mobile causally precedes the motion, since it is itself some cause of it. Therefore, even nature cannot posit a new world, since the mobile did not first precede the world in duration.

From this also it clearly follows that if one looks carefully at what we have already said, he cannot consider natural creation. For nature produces all its effects from subject matter and matter, but action from subject matter and matter is generation and not creation. Therefore, the natural cannot consider creation. For how does the natural consider that which does not extend to its own principles? And since the making of the world, or the production of it into being, cannot be generation, as is self-evident, but is creation, it follows from this that in no part of natural science is the making of the world or production into being taught, because that production is not natural, and therefore to does not belong to the natural

It also follows from what has been said that the natural man cannot from his own knowledge posit the first man, and the reason is that the nature of which the natural man intends can do nothing except by generation, and the first man cannot be generated. For man begets man and the sun. For the mode of becoming of the first man is different from that of generation, and it should not be surprising to anyone that he cannot consider those things to which the principles of his knowledge do not extend. For he who will carefully consider what he can naturally consider natural, it will appear to him that what has been said is reasonable: for not every artist can consider every truth.

But if you oppose, since this is the truth of the Christian faith and also the simple truth that the world is new and not eternal, and that creation is possible, and that there was the first man, and that the dead man will return alive without generation and the same number, and that he is the same man in number, who was already corruptible before, will be incorruptible, and thus in one species the atoms will be these two differences, corruptible and incorruptible, although the natural cannot cause or know these truths, because the principles of his knowledge are to such arduous and so hidden works of divine wisdom they do not extend themselves, yet he must not deny these truths. For although one artist cannot cause or know from his own principles the truths of the knowledge of other artists, he must not deny them. Therefore, although a naturalist cannot know these things which have been aforesaid from his own principles, nor assert them, because the principles of his knowledge do not extend to such things, yet he must not deny them, if another posits them, not as truths by reasons, but by a revelation made by some superior cause.

To this it must be said that he must not deny truths which the natural man cannot cause from his own principles nor know, but which nevertheless do not contradict his principles, nor destroy his knowledge: so that there are four possible right angles around any point marked on the surface, he has the truth. Nature cannot cause it from its own principles, nor must it deny it, because it does not contradict its own principles, nor does it destroy its own knowledge. However, that truth which he cannot cause or know from his principles, which nevertheless contradicts his principles and destroys his knowledge, he must deny, because just as a consequence from principles must be granted, so it is contradictory to deny: that a dead man immediately returns to life and becomes a thing that can be generated without generation - as the Christian, who posits the resurrection of the dead, must return in the same number - this must be denied by the natural, because the natural allows nothing, except what it sees to be possible through natural causes. But the Christian admits that these things are possible through a higher cause which is the cause of all nature, and therefore they do not contradict themselves in this, as in others.

But if you object further, since this is the truth that a dead man immediately returns alive and in the same number, as the Christian faith, which is most true in its articles, states, does not the natural negator say this is false?

It must be said that the first movement and the world are new [by superior causes], and yet it is not new by natural causes and natural principles. Thus, they stand together, if one looks carefully, that the world and the first movement are new and natural, denying the world and it is true to say that the first movement is new, because the natural denies that the world and the first movement are new just as the natural is, and this is to deny that it is new from natural principles. allows Hence the conclusion in which the naturalist says that the world and the first motion are not new, if taken absolutely, is false, but if it is referred to the reasons and principles from which he himself concludes it, it follows from them. For we know that he who says that Socrates is white, and he who denies that Socrates is white, in certain respects both say the truth. Thus, the Christian speaks the truth, when he says that the world and movement were first new, and that man was first, and that man should return alive and of the same number, and that a generable thing should be made without generation, when, however, it is granted that this is possible through a cause whose power is greater than the power of the cause. natural; but also says the naturalist who says that this is not possible from natural causes and principles: for the naturalist allows or denies nothing except from natural principles and causes, just as the grammarian also denies or allows nothing according to such things except from grammatical principles and causes. And since the naturalist, considering only the virtues of natural causes, says that the world and motion cannot first [be] new from them, whereas the Christian faith, considering a cause superior to nature, says that the world can be new from it, therefore they do not contradict in anything. Thus, two things are clear: one is that the natural does not contradict the Christian faith about the eternity of the world, and the other is that it cannot be shown by natural reasons that the world and its first movement were new.

8. But the fact that a mathematician cannot show this is clearly declared in this way: because astrology is one part of mathematics, and it has two parts: namely, one which teaches the different movements of the stars and their velocities, namely, which complete their course faster and slower, and the distances and

their connections and aspects and the like; Another part of the science of the stars is that which teaches the effects which they exert on the whole body which is under the globe. Because neither what the first part teaches, nor what the second part teaches, show that the world and motion were first new; it would be eternal. And for the same reason that has just been said, neither the second part of the science of the stars can show that the world and motion were first new, because from this the same as they have now, the stars could have motions and conjunctions and virtues, even if the world and motion were first eternal, then they could also produce similar effects in the lower world to those which they do just now, even if the world and the first movement were eternal, therefore not even the second part of the science of the stars can show that the first movement and the world are new.

As neither the first part, nor even the [second] part of the mathematical sciences, which is geometry, can show this. For this does not follow from the principles of geometry, because the opposite of the consequent can stand with the antecedent, that is, the first motion and the world being eternal can stand with the principles of geometry and all its conclusions. For given that this is false, that motion is the first and the world is eternal, will the principles of geometry be false because of this, such as "to draw a straight line from point to point", or even "a point is of which it is not a part", and other such things, or even of their own conclusions? It is clear that it is not. Would all [possible] passions be in the same way demonstrable in their substance and by the same causes, even if the world were eternal, as if the world were new? It is agreed that yes.

And I say the same thing about the third and fourth part of the mathematical sciences, which are arithmetic and music, and in the same way as was declared about geometry. And this is obvious to him who is advanced in these sciences and who knows that they are possible.

9. Now that not even a metaphysician can show that the world is new is clear as follows: the world depends on the divine will, just as on its own sufficient cause; but the metaphysician cannot demonstrate that any effect in duration can follow its sufficient cause, or that it can be postponed to its sufficient cause;

therefore the metaphysician cannot demonstrate that the world is coeternal with the divine will, that the world was made only by the divine.

Likewise, he who cannot demonstrate that this was the form of the divine will, that he willed from eternity to produce the world at the hour in which it was made, he cannot demonstrate that the world is new and coeternal with the divine will, because it was willed by the willing according to the form of the will; but the metaphysician cannot demonstrate that such a form of the divine will existed from eternity: for to say that a metaphysician can demonstrate this is not only a figment, but also, I believe, akin to [some] insanity: for where does man have the reason by which he perfectly investigates the divine will?

10. And from what has been said, a syllogism is composed: there is no question whose conclusion can be shown by reason, which the philosopher should not discuss and determine, as far as is possible by reason, as has been declared; but no philosopher can show by reason that the first movement and the world are new, because neither natural, nor mathematical, nor divine, as is clear from what has been said; ; because he who would demonstrate this would have to demonstrate the form of the divine will. And who will investigate it? That is why Aristotle says, in the book of Topics, that "there is a problem about which we have no opinion in either way, such as whether the world is eternal" or not. For there are many things in faith which cannot be demonstrated by reason, such as that the dead return the living, the same in number, and that a generable thing returns without generation; and he who does not believe in these is a heretic, but he who seeks to know by reason is a fool.

Therefore, since effects and works are from virtue, and virtue from substance, who dares to say that he knows perfectly through reason [the divine substance and all its virtue? He should say that he knows perfectly] all the immediate effects of God: how they are from him, whether from the new or from eternity, and how they are maintained in existence by him, and how they are in him. For in Him and from Him and through Him all things are made or are. And who is there who can adequately investigate this? And since there are many such things which faith posits, which cannot be investigated by human reason, therefore where reason fails, faith must supply it, which must be confessed to be a divine power over human knowledge. And for this reason, you should not disbelieve the articles of faith, because some of them cannot be demonstrated, because if you proceed in this way, you will stand in no law, because there is no law of which all the articles can be demonstrated.

Thus, it appears clearly that there is no contradiction between the Christian faith and the philosophy of the eternity of the world, if the aforesaid are carefully examined, as we shall also make clear, God helping us, in other questions, in which the Christian faith and philosophy will appear superficially and to men who consider less carefully to disagree.

We say, then, that the world is not eternal, but created anew, although this cannot be demonstrated by reasons, as was seen above, just as certain other things also which pertain to faith: for if they could be demonstrated, it would not be faith, but knowledge. Hence neither sophistical reason should be brought in place of faith, [as is self-evident,] nor dialectical reason, because it does not make a firm attitude, but only an opinion, and faith must be firmer than opinion, nor demonstrative reason, because then faith would only be about by what might be shown.

11. Then we must respond to the arguments brought forward on both sides, and first to the arguments which endeavor to prove the opposite of the truth, namely, that the world is coeternal with God.

> a. To the first. Everything that is incorruptible has the power to always exist, if you understand by this name incorruptible that, since it is a being, it cannot fail, nor through corruption - of which the Philosopher speaks at the end of the 1st Physique: "everything that corrupts will pass into this last", that is in matter, - nor even by corruption, taking the name more liberally than the Philosopher himself ever does, which corruption can fall on every being that has another cause, as far as it is of itself. For every effect, as long as it lasts, is preserved in being by some of its causes, as long as it appears to the inducer; But that which is maintained in existence by something else

can fail in so far as it is of itself. If incorruptible is understood in both of these ways, then the greater proposition is true which says: Everything incorruptible has the power to always exist; and thus, it is not incorruptible, nor is any being having another cause.

And you prove that what is born is incorruptible. It is true that corruption is opposed to generation, because just as generation is from matter, so corruption is opposed to itself into matter, that is, into the opposite and not into pure negation. If, however, something is begotten, it is not necessary that for this very reason it should be more liberally taken up by incorruptible corruption, which, of course, is not [into matter nor] into its opposite, but into pure negation, just as every caused being can be corrupted by the circumscribed power of the preserver. And the ancient philosophers called this preservation the golden chain, by which every being in its order is preserved by the first being, and the first being itself, as it has no cause before itself, so it has no preserver before itself. And since it has already been touched upon that every being [that is] on this side is first preserved in being by virtue of the first principle, therefore let this be declared more.

And first by the words of the authors. In the *Book of Causes* it is written thus: "The fixation and essence of all intelligence is through pure goodness, which is the first cause." By its essence he understands its production into being, and by its fixation he understands its duration. And if intelligence endures through the power of the first principle, then all other beings are much more so. And this agrees with what is written in the law: "from him and through him are all things."

Likewise, Plato, speaking in the person of the first principle to the intelligences themselves, says these words: "My will is more effective in guarding your eternity than your nature."

And the same is shown by reason. A being caused does not have the nature of itself to exist, because if it had the nature of itself to exist, it would not be caused by another, but what endures and is preserved in being by its own power and not by any other superior power, this has the nature of itself to exist. Therefore, no being caused to exist is preserved by itself. And therefore, just as all the beings that are on this side of the first principle are from it, so they are maintained in existence by it, and if the first principle took away its power from beings, beings would not exist at all. And this is what is written in the Book of Causes: "all the virtues are dependent on one first virtue, which is the virtue of the virtues." And Averroes, speaking about this first principle, says: "That cause is more worthy both in being and in virtue than all beings; for all beings do not acquire being and virtue except from that cause. Therefore, it is itself a being in itself and truth by itself, and all other beings [are] they are beings and truths by virtue of being and by virtue of its truth.

Likewise, the virtue which makes eternal duration is an infinite virtue, because if it were finite, then a greater virtue could be accepted; therefore, since there cannot be a greater duration than eternal duration, it would follow that a greater virtue would not make a greater duration than a lesser virtue, which is impossible. But in no being caused is infinite power, because everything is caused by transit, or received by action, and this is contrary to infinite power.

This is also proved by another. Because the power of the first mover is greater than the power of any subsequent mover, and nothing can be greater than the infinite, therefore in no caused being there is infinite power, nor eternal duration per se, but through the power of the first principle, whose power is per se eternal and infinite. And the reason is made clear: just as a greater duration cannot be taken from a duration that is always, so it must be that the power which makes a duration that is always or eternal must be such that it could not be taken as a greater power, and such alone is infinite power.

b. To answer the second reason. When you say: that is eternal which does not have any duration before it, I say that it is false. For though time is not before the world, yet eternity is before the world: for it is always. You say: that which has an eternal duration before it is never. I say that it is not necessary. For that new thing which has been made today has before it an eternal duration, because it is eternity itself which is always, and yet it cannot be said that it itself never is.

c. To the third reason we must say that, although a being, whose production is from a subject and matter, whether by generation, depends on a double power, that is, on the active power of its agent and on the power of its matter, for nothing is made of matter, except that to that it itself had a passive power, yet those whose action is neither generation nor from matter, they depend only on the sole power of the active principle, not of matter. For how can you say that it depends on the power of matter, the production of which is not from matter, as the world is? For it is evident to everyone that the party of the world could not be a generation. Hence, if there were no other way of becoming than generation, nothing would have been universally made. I say, therefore, that the world was made and was made anew, because it is not coeternal with God. And when you say: 'therefore, it could be done, I say what is true: it could be done only by the power of the agent, not of the subject and of matter'. And since it has already been touched upon in the solution that any effect depends sufficiently on the sole power of the agent, of which anyone would doubt, therefore this is declared thus:

Everything whose action depends on matter, if there is no matter, it is impossible to [exist] itself; The whole being that is on this side of the first principle is made because it has a cause, and I call that made being that has another of its production. If, therefore, every action depends on matter, and none from the sole power of the acting principle, and apart from the whole being which is on this side of the first principle there was no matter, it follows that the whole being, which is the first principle, would be impossible. Therefore, something has been done which is impossible to be done.

d. To answer the fourth reason. When you say: Every new thing is made by transmutation, this is true only of beings whose creation is by generation: for transmutation is found only in things that can be generated. Hence the heavenly bodies which have innate substances, as they are transmuted according to their position, so are they generated according to their position.

e. To the fifth reason. When you say: everything is new in time, since the new must be made in some duration in some part of it, since if it were at the same time with any part of that duration, it would not be new in that duration, and the only duration that has parts is time, I mean to This is that something can be said to be new in two ways: either because it is when it was not before, but by having its being after its contradictory, not because it is in some part of the duration in which it is, and not in another. and thus, the world is new, and such a new need not be in time. In another way, something can be called new, because in some part of the duration in which it is, it has existence, in another part it has non-existence; and everything that is thus new is necessarily in time, because the only duration that has parts is time; and so, the world is not new. Hence the world cannot be new in any duration: not in time, because the world began with time, therefore no part of time precedes the world; nor in eternity, because eternity is indivisible, and what is in eternity always exists in one way.

f. To answer the sixth reason. When you say: every generation is from corruption, it is true. When you say, secondly, that every corruptible thing is first generated, I say that the naturalist allows this proposition, because he cannot, from his own principles, posit the aspect of a thing that is generable and corruptible except by generation. However, he who maintains that the aspect of a thing that can be generated is not through generation, just as he must maintain that he who puts man first - for man is a thing that can be generated, and his production cannot be through generation, if he is the first - he must deny that proposition which says: everything corrupt is first generated, because it contradicts its own position; for the first man was sometimes corrupted, although he was never begotten. Hence the sixth reason is based on natural principles, and it was said above that he who posits that the world is a new creation must let go of natural causes and seek a higher cause.

g. To answer the seventh reason. When you say that an effect in its duration cannot follow its sufficient cause, we say that this is true of a cause acting by nature, not of an agent acting voluntarily. For just as God can understand new things with his eternal intellect, even though they are not new with respect to himself, so he can act in a new way with his eternal will.

h. To answer the eighth reason. What the powerful and willing does of necessity, this is true in the hour to which the will is determined. Just so, although the power of God by which He was able to make the world, and the will by which He willed, is eternal, because that will was only with respect to the hour in which the world was made, therefore the world is new, although the will of God is eternal.

i. To answer another reason. When you say: every new effect requires some novelty in some of its principles, I mean that this is not necessary in the agent through the will, because according to the old will new actions can be done apart from the fact that a change has taken place in the will or in the willing. To confirm the reason, we must say that the agent was not only able to produce a new effect because he himself has a new substance, or because he himself has some new power or position, or because he was previously subject to an obstacle, or because in his passive from which he acts, a new thing has become disposition, but also some agent can produce a new effect by the fact that he himself has an eternal will determined for a certain hour in which he wishes to act, according to that will.

j. To the following reason it must be said that everything that moves after rest must not be reduced to eternal motion, but that everything that moves after rest must be reduced to first motion as if to some cause of its own which is not after rest. Hence, although the first movement is new, it is not itself after rest: for not every immobility is rest, but the immobility of that which was born to be moved, as it is written in *Physics III*. And before the first movement there was no mobile born to be moved, and I mean before in duration.

k. To answer another reason. When you say: the will which postpones the willed, waits for something in the future, it is true only of the will whose action is in time, because futurity and expectation are only in time, but of the will whose action is before time, this is not true; and the action of the divine will is prior to time, at least that by which it operated the world and time.

l. To the following reason we must say that those two which are in the same duration are together, if no part of that duration falls between them, just as two temporal things are together in time between which no part of time falls; If, however, there is no duration between any two, because one is in the now of eternity and the other is in the now of time, and thus no duration falls between them, it is not necessary that they should be such at the same time. Thus is the will of God which is in the now of eternity, and the action of the world which is in the now of time.

m. To answer another reason, as was said. You argue to the contrary, because to posit such a form of will in God is to imagine. It must be said that it is not true: for not all things are fictions which cannot be demonstrated.

As to what you argue in the second place, I say that from the time when such a form of the divine will was from eternity, such was the manner of proceeding of the willed of the will, so that the willed was perfectly conformable to the will.

n. To answer the following reason. When you say: from the old will, between which the transmutation does not fall and its effect, no new effect can take place, this alone is true of the will from which the effect proceeds by transmutation; such is not the divine will.

o. To another I say that this example is in some respects appropriate, though not perfectly.

Reasons for the opposing party are granted by the conclusion, although they can be resolved, since they are sophisticated.

12. From these, then, it appears that for a philosopher to say that something is possible or impossible is this: to say that it is possible or impossible according to reasons that can be investigated by man. For as soon as one dismisses reason, he ceases to be a philosopher, and philosophy does not rest on revelations and miracles. Since then, you yourself say and must say that there are many truths, which, however, if you do not affirm the truths except as far as human reason can lead you, you must never admit them, as is the resurrection of men which faith posits. And in such cases, it is good that divine authority is believed and not human reason. For I ask you: what reason shows this? Let me also ask: what reason shows that a generable thing after its corruption can return again without generation, and also the same in number as it was before its corruption, as must happen in the resurrection of men according to the opinion of our faith? However, the philosopher says at the end of De generation 2 that a corrupted thing can return the same in kind, but not the same in number. Nor for this reason does he contradict faith, because he himself says that this is not possible according to natural causes. For it is from such things that the natural is reasoned. But our faith says that this is possible through a superior cause which is the beginning and end of our faith, God be the glorious and blessed.

13. Therefore there is no contradiction between faith and philosophy. Why, then, do you grumble against the philosopher, when you admit the same thing as him? And do not believe that the philosopher who devoted his life to the

study of wisdom contradicted the truth of the Catholic faith in anything, but study more, because you have a little understanding with respect to the philosophers who were and are the wise men of the world, so that you can understand their words. For the words of the teacher must be understood for the better, and it is not worth what some malicious people say, who place their interest in the fact that they can find reasons that are inconsistent with some truth of the Christian faith, which, however, is beyond doubt impossible. For they say that a Christian cannot be a philosopher, as such, because he is compelled by his own law to destroy the principles of philosophy. For this is false, because the Christian admits that a conclusion concluded by philosophical reasons cannot be otherwise than that by which it is concluded, and if it is concluded by natural causes. The fact that the dead will not return alive immediately with the same number, this admits that it cannot have otherwise by the natural causes by which it is concluded; yet he admits that this can be otherwise through a higher cause which is the cause of the whole nature and of the whole being caused. Therefore, the Christian, who is thoroughly intelligent, is not compelled by his law to destroy the principles of philosophy but saves both faith and philosophy by correcting neither. But if a man, established in a position of dignity or not, and cannot understand such arduous things, then he should obey the wiser and believe the Christian law, not because of the sophistic reason, because it errs, nor because of the dialectical reason, because it does not make for such a firm attitude as faith does. because the conclusion of the dialectical reason is accepted with fear of the other part, and not by demonstrative reason, both because it is not possible in all that our law lays down, and also because it itself makes knowledge. "For demonstration is the making of a syllogism to know," as is written in *Posterior I*, and faith is not knowledge. Hence every Christian must adhere to the law of Christ and believe according to what the author of the same law, the glorious Christ, who is the blessed God forever and ever, must do. Amen.

LATIN TEXT

1. Quia sicut in his quae ex lege credi debent, quae tamen pro se rationem non habent, quaerere rationem stultum est, quia qui hoc facit, quaerit quod impossibile est inveniri, - et eis nolle credere sine ratione haereticum est, sic in his quae non sunt manifesta de se, quae tamen pro se rationem habent, eis velle credere sine ratione philosophicum non est, ideo - volentes sententiam christianae fidei de aeternitate mundi et sententiam Aristotelis et quorundam aliorum philosophorum reducere ad concordiam, ut sententia fidei firmiter teneatur quamquam in quibusdam demonstrari non possit, - ne incurramus stultitiam, quaerendo demonstrationem ubi ipsa non est possibilis, ne etiam incurramus haeresim, nolentes credere quod ex fide teneri debet, quia pro se demonstrationem non habet, sicut fuit mos quibusdam philosophis quibus nulla lex posita placuit, quia articuli legis positae pro se non habebant demonstrationem, ut etiam sententia philosophorum salvetur, quantum ratio eorum concludere potest, - nam eorum sententia in nullo contradicit christianae fidei nisi apud non intelligentes: sententia enim philosophorum innititur demonstrationibus et certis rationibus possibilibus in rebus de quibus loquuntur, fides autem in multis, innititur miraculis et non rationibus: quod enim tenetur propter hoc quod per rationes conclusum est, non est fides sed scientia, - et ut appareat quod fides et philosophia sibi non contradicunt de aeternitate mundi, ut etiam pateat quod rationes quorundam haereticorum non habent vigorem per quas contra christianam fidem mundum tenent esse aeternum, de hoc per rationem inquiramus, scilicet utrum mundus sit aeternus.

2. Et videtur quod non: primum principium est causa substantiae mundi, quia si non, tunc plura essent prima principia; quod autem habet esse ab alio, hoc sequitur illud in duratione, ergo mundus sequitur primum principium in duratione; ens autem aeternum nullum sequitur in duratione; ergo mundus non est aeternus.

Item, nihil potest Deo adaequari; si ergo mundus esset aeternus, mundus adaequaretur Deo in duratione; hoc autem est impossibile; ergo, etc.

Item, virtus finita non potest facere durationem infinitam, quia duratio non excedit virtutem facientem ipsam; virtus autem caeli finita est, sicut et virtus cuiuslibet corporis finiti; ergo virtus caeli non facit durationem aeternam, ergo caelum non est aeternum, ergo nec totus mundus, cum mundus non praecedat caelum.

Item, Deus praecedit mundum secundum naturam, in Deo autem idem est natura et duratio; ergo Deus praecedit mundum secundum durationem. Ergo mundus non est aeternus.

Item, omne creatum est ex nihilo factum: in hoc enim differunt creatio et generatio, quia generatio omnis est ex subiecto et materia: ideo generans non potest in totam substantiam rei; creatio autem non est ex subiecto et materia, et ideo creans potest in totam substantiam rei. Mundus autem est creatus, quia ante mundum non erat subiectum et materia ex qua fieret mundus, ergo mundus est ex nihilo: tale autem est ens postquam fuit non ens; cum igitur simul non potuit esse ens et non-ens, ergo prius fuit non-ens et postmodum ens; sed omne illud quod habet esse post non-esse, illud est novum; mundus igitur est novus, ergo non est aeternus, cum novum et aeternum non se compatiantur in eodem.

Item, cui potest fieri additio, illo potest aliquid esse maius; toti tempori quod praecessit, potest fieri additio temporis, ergo et toto tempore quod praecessit potest esse aliquid maius; infinito autem nihil potest esse maius, ergo totum tempus quod praecessit non est infinitum; ergo neque motus, nec mundus.

Item, si mundus esset aeternus, tunc generatio animalium et plantarum et corporum simplicium esset aeterna; ergo individuum demonstratum esset ex infinitis causis generantibus: quia, si generatio esset aeterna, tunc hoc individuum hominis praecederet aliud, et illud aliud, et sic in infinitum; unum autem effectum esse ex infinitis causis agentibus est imposibile: quoniam, si non sit primum agens vel movens, non est motus, quia primum movens est causa totius motus, ut scribitur II Metaphysicae, et de se patet, inter autem infinita agentia nullum potest esse primum; ergo haec generatio non est aeterna, ergo neque mundus.

Item, vult Aristoteles VI Physicorum quod eiusdem rationis est magnitudo, motus et tempus, quantum ad finitatem et infinitatem; cum igitur nulla magnitudo sit infinita, sicut probat Aristoteles III Physicorum, ergo nec motus est infinitus, nec tempus, ergo nec mundus: cum mundus non sit sine istis.

Item, si mundus esset aeternus, tunc infiniti homines essent generati et corrupti, homine autem corrupto manet substantia quae in corpore erat, anima [scilicet] rationalis, cum ipsa sit ingenerabilis et incorruptibilis, et sic tales substantiae infinitae essent simul in actu; infinita autem esse [simul] in actu est impossibile; ergo etc.

Item, si mundus esset aeternus, tunc motus infinitus esset pertransitus et infinitum tempus, quia, si mundus esset aeternus, tunc tempus praecedens hoc instans esset infinitum; sed infinitum esse pertransitum et acceptum est impossibile; ergo, etc.

Item, quod habet causam aliam, hoc habet initium; mundus habet causam aliam: ergo mundus habet initium; "mare enim factum est, quia mundus factus est", sicut dicitur II Meteororum; quod habet initium, non est aeternum; ergo, etc.

3. In contrarium arguitur, et primo: quod mundus possit esse aeternus, et quod ex hoc nullum sequatur impossibile; secundo ostenditur quod mundus sit aeternus. Primum sic: licet effectus sequatur suam causam naturaliter, potest tamen simul esse cum sua causa in duratione; mundus et totum ens causatum est effectus primi entis; ergo, cum primum ens sit aeternum, mundus potest sibi esse coeternus. Maior patet, quia prioritas et posterioritas naturae et simultas durationis compatiuntur se. Minor etiam patet, quia, sicut in omni genere oportet quod primum sit causa omnium aliorum, sic et in genere entis oportet quod primum ens sit causa aliorum, et ex hoc sequitur quod illud primum ens sit ens non causatum, quoniam ipsum debet esse causa sufficiens rerum; sed nulla res causata est sufficiens causa alicuius sui effectus, quoniam a quo dependet essentia entis causati, ab eodem dependet omnis eius effectus, ergo

primum ens oportet esse ens non habens aliam causam: aliter enim primum ens non esset.

Hoc idem, apparet per Aristotelem VIII Physicorum, qui dicit quod, licet aliquid sit aeternum, non tamen debet poni principium: triangulum enim habere tres angulos aequales duobus rectis est aeternum, huius tamen aeterni quaerenda est altera causa; ergo aeternum potest habere causam; cum igitur nihil in duratione potest praecedere illud quod est aeternum, igitur effectus potest esse coaeternus suae causae; mundus est effectus primi entis; ergo mundus potest esse sibi coaeternus.

Item, patet per exemplum: si sol semper fuisset in nostro haemisphaerio, lumen semper fuisset in medio, et fuisset lumen coaeternum soli, et tamen effectus eius; quod non esset, nisi effectus posset esse simul cum sua causa in duratione.

Item, si pes semper fuisset in pulvere, vestigium sibi fuisset coaeternum, et tamen effectus eius.

Item, hoc idem arguitur per rationem sic: nihil est aeternum in futuro absque praeterito, quia virtus quae potest facere durationem aeternam alicuius rei in futuro, ipsa potest fecisse durationem aeternam eiusdem rei in praeterito: cum illa virtus sit intransmutabilis et semper se uno modo habens; mundus autem est aeternus in futuro et secundum sententiam christianae fidei, et secundum quorundam philosophorum opinionem; ergo per eandem virtutem potuit fuisse aeternus in praeterito. Sic ergo mundus potest esse aeternus, et ex hoc nullum videtur sequi impossibile per rationem, nec ex hoc potest argumentari aliquod inconveniens. Et hoc apparebit illi qui studium suum posuerit ad hoc.

4. Quod autem mundus sit aeternus, arguitur sic:

<1> Omne incorruptibile habet virtutem ut sit semper; quia si talem virtutem non haberet, incorruptibile non esset. Mundus autem est incorruptibilis, quia omne ingenitum est incorruptibile; ergo mundus habet virtutem ut sit semper;

res autem per totam durationem ad quam virtus sua essendi se extendit: ergo mundus est aeternus.

<2> Item, illud est aeternum quod non habet ante se aliquam durationem: omne enim novum habet ante se aliquam durationem; sed mundus ante se nullam habuit durationem, quoniam non tempus: tempus enim non erat ante mundum, quia tempus sequitur motum primi mobilis, ut passio subiectum; neque erat aeternitas ante mundum, quoniam illud nunquam est quod habet ante se aeternam durationem; si ergo ante mundum fuisset aeterna duratio, mundus nunquam fuisset.

<3> Item, quod fit de novo, hoc potest fieri, quia si non, tunc fieret quod impossibile est fieri; quo autem res potest fieri, haec est materia; sed ante mundi factionem non erat aliqua materia ex qua mundus fieret; ergo mundus non est de novo factus, ergo est aeternus: cum inter novum et aeternum non sit medium.

<4> Item, omne novum factum est per transmutationem; quoniam qui tollit transmutationem, tollit omnem novitatem; omnis autem transmutatio habet subiectum et materiam, ut scribitur principio VIII Metaphysicae et VII eiusdem et III Physicorum: quoniam motus et omnis mutatio est actus entis in potentia [et quidem] secundum quod huiusmodi; cum igitur ante mundum non fuerit aliqua materia et subiectum transmutationis quae exigeretur ad novam factionem mundi, si mundus esset factum novum; ergo mundus non est novum factum, sed aeternum.

<5> Item, omne novum est in tempore, quoniam novum in aliqua duratione, oportet quod fiat in parte illius: quod enim fit in toto die, non est novum in die, et quod est in toto anno, illud non est novum in anno, sed illud quod est novum in anno oportet quod sit in aliqua parte anni, inter autem durationes omnes solum tempus partes habet; mundus autem naturaliter est ante tempus; ergo mundus non est novus, sed aeternus.

<6> Item, omnis generatio est ex corrupto, et omne corruptum est prius generatum; similiter omnis corruptio est ex generato, et omne generatum est ex corrupto; ergo ante omnem generationem est generatio, et ante omnem corruptionem est corruptio; ergo non convenit dare primam generationem nec primam corruptionem, ergo generatio et corruptio est aeterna; ergo mundus est aeternus, quia quae generantur et corrumpuntur sunt partes mundi quae non possunt praecedere mundum in duratione.

<7> Item, effectus suam causam sufficientem non potest sequi in duratione. Causa sufficiens mundi est aeterna, quia ipsa est primum principium; ergo mundus non potest ipsam sequi in duratione; quia primum principium est aeternum, ergo mundus est sibi coaeternus. Et confirmatur ratio: ens aeternum, et secundum suam substantiam, et secundum omnem suam dispositionem, cui nihil acquisitum est in futuro, et cui nihil deficit in praeterito ex his per quae effectum suum produceret, facit effectum suum immediatum sibi coaeternum; Deus est ens aeternum secundum substantiam et secundum omnem, quaecunque in eo est, dispositionem, cui nihil acquisitum est in futuro, [et cui] nihil deficit in praeterito ex his per quae effectum suum produceret, et mundus est suus effectus immediatus; ergo mundus est Deo coeternus.

<8> Item, Aristoteles dicit in IX Metaphysicae quod "agens per voluntatem, cum potest et vult, tunc agit, nec oportet addere, si non sit impeditum: quoniam posse removet impedimentum"; sed Deus ab aeterno habuit potentiam et voluntatem faciendi mundum; ergo mundus est factum aeternum.

<9> Item, omnis effectus novus aliquam novitatem requirit in aliquo suorum principiorum: quoniam, si omnia principia alicuius effectus semper se haberent uno modo, ex eis non posset fieri effectus, cum prius non esset; sed in principio mundi, - quod est ens primum -, nulla est novitas possibilis; ergo mundus non est effectus novus. Et confirmatur ratio: aliquod agens, si ipsum est novum secundum substantiam suam, ipsum potest esse causa novi effectus, aut quia ipsum est aeternum secundum substantiam, novum tamen secundum aliquam virtutem vel situm - sicut apparet in corpore caeli - aut quia prius subiacebat impedimento, aut quia in subiecto ex quo agit, facta est nova dispositio; in

causa mundi nullum istorum est possibile, ut de se apparet; ergo mundus non est causatum novum.

<10> Item, omne quod movetur post quietem, reducitur ad motum continuum qui semper est: quoniam quod aliquid quandoque moveatur, quandoque quiescit, non potuit contingere ex causa immobili; cum igitur in motibus non poterit procedere in infinitum, quorum unus est causa alterius; ergo oportet primum motum esse continuum et aeternum. Et propter hanc rationem Aristoteles VIII Physicorum omnem motum novum reducit ad motum primum, sicut ad causam suam, qui secundum opinionem suam est aeternus; et hanc opinionem tenet Aristoteles propter hanc rationem. Motus qui semper habet causas sufficientes, non potest esse novus; sed primus motus habet semper causas sufficientes; quia, si non, tunc ipsum praecessisset alius motus, per quem facta esset sufficientia in causis suis, cum prius non esset, ergo ipse esset primus et non-primus, quod est impossibile.

<11> Item, voluntas quae postponit volitum, aliquid exspectat in futuro; ante mundum non est aliqua exspectatio: quia ante mundum non est tempus, et nulla exspectatio est nisi in tempore; ergo mundus non est postpositus voluntati divinae, illa autem est aeterna, ergo mundus voluntati divinae est coaeternus.

<12> Item, omnis effectus qui sufficienter dependet ab aliqua voluntate inter quem et ipsam voluntatem nulla cadit duratio, simul est cum illa voluntate: quia simul sunt in duratione, inter quae nulla cadit duratio, sed mundus sufficienter dependet a voluntate divina, - aliam enim causam non habet - et inter illa nulla cadit duratio, quia non tempus; ante mundum enim non erat tempus nec aeternitas, quia tunc nonesse mundi esset in aeternitate; cum igitur illud est aeternum quod est in aeternitate, tunc nonesse mundi esset aeternum; ergo mundus nunquam esset quod est impossibile, ergo mundus coaeternus est voluntati divinae.

<13> Item, omnis effectus novus ante se requirit aliquam transmutationem vel in agente suo, vel in subiecto ex quo fit, vel saltem illam quae est adventus horae

in qua agens, semper uno modo se habens, vult agere; ante mundum nulla potuit esse transmutatio; ergo mundus non potest esse effectus novus.

5. Respondebit aliquis quod immo mundus est factum novum, quia haec fuit forma voluntatis divinae ab aeterno, ut mundum produceret in hora in qua factus est: ab antiqua enim voluntate potest procedere effectus novus, et propter hoc non oportet quod contingat aliqua transmutatio vel in voluntate vel in volente: habet enim aliquis nunc voluntatem faciendi aliquid post tres dies, adveniente tertia die facit tunc quod prius voluit et ab antiquo, nec tamen facta est aliqua transmutatio in voluntate nec in volente; et hoc modo mundus potest esse novus, quamquam habet causam aeternam [et] sufficientem.

Sed contra hunc modum ponendi arguitur sic: qui fingit antecedens, fingit omne, quod ex ipso sequitur, nec ipsum certificat; tu autem fingis in Deo talem formam voluntatis ab aeterno, nec eam potes declarare, et sic facile est omnia fingere: dicet enim tibi aliquis quod non fuit talis forma divinae voluntatis ab aeterno, nec habes, unde sibi contradicas; ergo etiam fingis mundum esse novum, nec hoc poteris declarare.

Item, contra eundem modum ponendi arguitur sic: volitum procedit a voluntate secundum formam voluntatis; si ergo talis fuit forma voluntatis divinae quod ab aeterno voluit producere mundum in hora, ut tu dicis, ergo fuisset Deo impossibile prius mundum produxisse quod videtur inconveniens, cum Deus sit agens per libertatem voluntatis.

Ad hanc rationem respondebis quod, immo Deus potuit prius fecisse mundum, quia, sicut habuit hanc formam voluntatis ab aeterno, sic potuit habere aliam, et ideo, sicut mundum produxit in hora in qua factus est, sic potuit ipsum prius produxisse.

Sed contra hanc rationem arguitur sic: quod unius formae voluntatis est et potest esse alterius, hoc est transmutabile secundum voluntates; sed Deus penitus est intransmutabilis; ergo non potest habere aliam formam voluntatis quam illam quam habuit ab aeterno.

<14> Item, ab antiqua voluntate, inter quam et suum effectum non cadit transmutatio, non potest fieri novus effectus: quod enim effectus non est simul cum causa in duratione, hoc facit transmutatio cadens inter illa: qui enim transmutationem tollit, ipse tollit omnem exspectationem; sed inter voluntatem Dei, quae aeterna est et mundum nulla potest cadere transmutatio; ergo ante mundum nulla potest esse transmutatio; ergo mundus coaeternus est voluntati divinae.

<15> Item, secundum exemplum quod positum est, non est conveniens in proposito; scilicet quod homo aliquis nunc habet voluntatem faciendi aliquid post tres dies, adveniente autem tertia die facit illud quod ab antiquo voluit, illud exemplum inconveniens est in proposito: quia, licet in voluntate non sit facta transmutatio nec in volente, tamen facta est transmutatio quae est adventus horae, scilicet tertiae diei. Quodsi nec facta esset transmutatio in volente, nec in passivo ex quo fieri debuit novus effectus; nec illa transmutatio quae est adventus horae, tunc ex aliqua voluntate non posset fieri novus effectus, quia omnis novus effectus requirit ante se aliquam transmutationem, ut diceret aliquis. Et quia ante mundum non est facta transmutatio in voluntate ex qua factus est mundus, nec in materia ex qua fieri deberet mundus - quoniam mundum non antecedit materia - nec etiam facta est illa transmutatio ante mundum quae est adventus alicuius horae, tunc videtur quod ex voluntate aeterna non potuerit fieri mundus novus. Et ideo illud exemplum inconveniens est in proposito.

Istae sunt rationes per quas quidam haeretici, tenentes aeternitatem mundi nituntur impugnare sententiam christianae fidei, quae ponit mundum esse novum; contra quas expedit, ut christianus studeat diligenter, ut sciat eas perfecte solvere, si haereticus aliquis eas opponat. Haec sunt rationes:

Solutio

6. Primo hic diligenter considerandum est quod nulla quaestio [potest esse quae] disputabilis est per rationes, quam philosophus non debeat disputare et determinare, quomodo se habeat veritas in illa, quantum per rationem

humanam comprehendi potest. Et huius declaratio est, quia omnes rationes per quas disputatur, ex rebus acceptae sunt: aliter enim essent figmentum intellectus; philosophus autem omnium rerum naturas docet: sicut enim philosophia docet ens, sic partes philosophiae docent partes entis, ut scribitur IV Metaphysicae, et de se patet; ergo philosophus omnem quaestionem per rationem disputabilem habet determinare: omnis enim quaestio disputabilis per ratione cadit in aliqua parte entis, philosophus autem omne ens speculatur: naturale, mathematicum et divinum; ergo omnem quaestionem per rationes disputabilem habet philosophus determinare, et qui contrarium dicit, sciat se proprium sermonem ignorare.

Secundo est notandum quod nec naturalis, nec mathematicus, nec metaphysicus potest ostendere per rationes motum primum et mundum novum esse.

7. Quod autem naturalis non potest hoc ostendere, declaratur sic accipiendo duas suppositiones per se notas, quarum prima est: quod nullus artifex potest aliquid causare, concedere vel negare nisi ex principiis suae scientiae. Secunda suppositio est: quod, quamvis natura non sit primum principium simpliciter, est tamen primum principium in genere rerum naturalium, et primum principium quod naturalis considerare potest. Et ideo Aristoteles hoc considerans in libro Physicorum, qui est primus liber doctrinae naturalium, incepit non a primo principio simpliciter, sed a primo principio rerum naturalium, scilicet a materia prima, quam in II eiusdem dicit esse naturam. Ex his autem ad propositum.

Natura non potest causare aliquem motum novum, nisi ipsum praecedat alius motus qui sit causa eius; sed primum motum non potest alius motus praecedere, quia tunc ipse non esset primus motus; ergo naturalis, cuius primum principium est natura, non potest ponere secundum sua principia primum motum esse novum. Maior patet, quia natura materialis nihil agit de novo nisi prius agatur ab alio: natura enim materialis non potest esse primus motor. Quomodo enim ens genitum erit primus motor? Et omne agens materiale est ens genitum. Nec est instantia de corpore caeli, quia si sit ens materiale, tamen non habet materiam univoce cum rebus generabilibus;

transmutabilia enim sunt ad invicem quae materiam unius naturae communicant.

Item, omnis effectus naturalis novus aliquam requirit novitatem in suis immediatis principiis; novitas autem non potest esse in aliquo ente sine transmutatione praecedente: qui enim tollit transmutationem, ipse tollet novitatem; ergo natura nullum motum vel effectum novum causare potest sine transmutatione praecedente. Ideo secundum naturalem, cuius primum principium est natura, motus primus, quem nulla transmutatio praecedere potest, non potest esse novus. Maior patet, quia, si omnia principia immediata alicuius effectus naturalis semper fuissent in eadem dispositione, ex eis non posset ille effectus nunc esse, cum prius non esset. Quaeram enim, quare magis nunc quam prius, nec habes, unde respondebis. Dico autem in hac ratione "principia immediata", quia, licet effectus naturalis sit novus, non propter hoc oportet quod in suis principiis mediatis et primis facta sit aliqua transmutatio et novitas. Quamvis enim proxima principia rerum generabilium transmutantur et quandoque sunt, et quandoque non sunt, primae tamen causae earum semper sunt.

Ex his apparet manifeste quod naturalis non potest ponere aliquem motum novum, nisi ipsum praecedat aliquis motus qui sit causa eius; ergo, cum necesse sit in mundo ponere aliquem motum primum -, non enim contingit abire in infinitum in motibus quorum unus sit causa alterius - sequitur quod naturalis ex sua scientia et suis principiis quibus ipse utitur, non potest ponere primum motum novum.

Ideo quod Aristoteles VIII Physicorum quaerens utrum motus aliquando factus sit, cum prius non esset, et utens his principiis, quae modo dicta sunt, et loquens ut naturalis, ponit motum primum aeternum ex utraque parte. Ipse etiam in eodem VIII Physicorum quaerens, quare quaedam quandoque moventur, quandoque quiescunt, respondet quod hoc est, quia moventur a motore semper moto. Quia enim motor a quo moventur, est motor motus, ideo diversimode se habet, propter hoc facit sua mobilia quandoque moveri et quandoque quiescere. Illa autem quae semper moventur, ut corpora caeli, moventur a motore immobili, semper uno modo se habente in se et ad sua mobilia.

Si ergo naturalis non potest secundum sua principia ponere motum primum novum, ergo nec ipsum mobile [primum], quia mobile causaliter praecedit motum, cum ipsum sit aliqua causa eius. Ergo nec naturalis potest ponere mundum novum, cum mobile primum non praecessit mundum in duratione.

Ex hoc etiam contingit manifeste quod si quis diligenter inspexerit quae iam diximus, quod naturalis creationem considerare non potest. Natura enim omnem suum effectum facit ex subiecto et materia, factio autem ex subiecto et materia generatio est et non creatio. Ideo naturalis creationem considerare non potest. Quomodo enim naturalis illud considerat quod ad sua principia non se extendunt? Et cum factio mundi, sive productio eius in esse non possit esse generatio, ut de se patet, sed est creatio, ex hoc contingit quod in nulla parte scientiae naturalis factio mundi sive productio in esse docetur, quia illa productio naturalis non est et ideo ad naturalem non pertinet.

Ex his etiam, quae dicta sunt, contingit quod naturalis ex sua scientia non potest ponere primum hominem, et ratio est, quia natura de qua intendit naturalis, nihil potest facere nisi per generationem, et primus homo non potest esse generatus. Homo enim generat hominem et sol. Modus enim fiendi primi hominis alius est quam per generationem, nec debet esse mirabile alicui quod naturalis non potest illa considerare ad quae principia suae scientiae se non extendunt. Qui enim diligenter considerabit quae per se potest naturalis considerare, illi apparebit rationabile esse quod dictum est: non enim cuilibet artifex considerare potest quamlibet veritatem.

Si autem opponas, cum haec sit veritas christianae fidei et etiam veritas simpliciter quod mundus sit novus et non aeternus, et quod creatio sit possibilis, et quod primus homo erat, et quod homo mortuus redibit vivus sine generatione et idem numero, et quod ille idem homo in numero qui iam ante erat corruptibilis, erit incorruptibilis, et sic in una specie atoma erunt istae duae differentiae corruptibile et incorruptibile, quamvis naturalis istas veritates causare non possit nec scire, eo quod principia suae scientiae ad tam ardua et tam occulta opera sapientiae divinae non se extendunt, tamen istas veritates negare non debet. Licet enim unus artifex non possit causare vel scire ex suis principiis veritates scientiarum aliorum artificum, non tamen eas negare debet. Ergo, licet naturalis haec quae praedicta sunt, ex suis principiis scire non possit, nec asserere, eo quod principia suae scientiae ad talia se non extendunt, non tamen debet ea negare, si alius ea ponat, non tamen tanquam vera per rationes, sed per revelationem factam ab aliqua causa superiori.

Dicendum est ad hoc quod veritates quas naturalis non potest causare ex suis principiis nec scire, quae tamen non contrariantur suis principiis, nec destruunt suam scientiam, negare non debet: ut quod circa quemlibet punctum signatum in superficie sunt quattuor recti anguli possibiles, habeat veritatem, naturalis ex suis principiis causare non potest, nec tamen debet eam negare, quia non contrariatur suis principiis, nec destruit suam scientiam. Veritatem tamen illam quam ex suis principiis causare non potest nec scire, quae tamen contrariatur suis principiis et destruit suam scientiam, negare debet, quia sicut consequens ex principiis est concedendum, sic repugnans est negandum: ut hominem mortuum immediate redire vivum et rem generabilem fieri sine generatione - ut ponit christianus, qui ponit resurrectionem mortuorum, ut debeat et corruptum redire idem numero - ista debet negare naturalis, quia naturalis nihil concedit, nisi quod videt esse possibile per causas naturales. Christianus autem concedit haec esse possibilia per causam superiorem quae est causa totius naturae, ideo sibi non contradicunt in hic, sicut nec in aliis.

Si autem ulterius opponas, cum haec sit veritas quod homo mortuus immediate redit vivus et idem numero, sicut ponit fides christiana quae in suis articulis verissima est, nonne naturalis negans hoc dicit falsum?

Dicendum ad hoc quod simul stant motum primum et mundum esse novum [per causas superiores], et tamen non esse novum per causas naturales et principia naturalia, sic simul stant, si quis diligenter inspiciat, mundum et motum primum esse novum et naturalem negantem mundum et motum primum esse novum dicere verum, quia naturalis negat mundum et motum primum esse novum sicut naturalis, et hoc est ipsum negare ex principiis naturalibus esse novum: quicquid enim naturalis, secundum quod naturalis, negat vel concedit, ex causis et principiis naturalibus hoc negat vel concedit. Unde conclusio in qua naturalis dicit mundum et primum motum non esse novum, accepta absolute, falsa est, sed si referatur in rationes et principia ex quibus ipse eam concludit, ex illis sequitur. Scimus enim quod qui dicit Socratem esse album et qui negat Socratem esse album, secundum quaedam uterque dicit verum. Sic verum dicit christianus, dicens mundum et motum primum esse novum, et primum hominem fuisse, et hominem redire vivum et eundem numero, et rem generabilem fieri sine generatione, cum tamen hoc concedatur possibile esse per causam cuius virtus est maior, quam sit virtus causae naturalis; verum etiam dicit naturalis qui dicit hoc non esse possibile ex causis et principiis naturalibus: nam naturalis nihil concedit vel negat nisi ex principiis et causis naturalibus, sicut etiam nihil negat vel concedit grammaticus secundum quod huiusmodi nisi ex principiis et causis grammaticalibus. Et quia naturalis solum considerans virtutes causarum naturalium, dicit mundum et motum primum non [posse esse] novum, ex eis, fides autem christiana, considerans causam superiorem quam sit natura, dicit mundum posse esse novum ex illa, ideo non contradicunt in aliquo. Sic ergo patent duo: unum est quod naturalis non contradicit christianae fidei de aeternitate mundi, et aliud est quod per rationes naturales non potest ostendi mundum et motum primum esse novum.

8. Quod autem mathematicus hoc non possit ostendere, sic declaratur manifeste: quia mathematicarum una pars est astrologia, et ipsa habet duas partes: unam scilicet quae docet diversos motus stellarum et velocitates earum, quae scilicet velocius et tardius complent cursum suum, et distantias et coniunctiones et aspectus earum et caetera talia; alia pars scientiae astrorum est quae docet effectus quos agunt in toto corpore quod sub orbe est. Quia nec illa quae docet pars prima, nec quae docet pars secunda, ostendunt mundum et motum primum esse novum, quia tales possunt esse tarditates et velocitates quarundam stellarum in suis sphaeris respectu aliarum et etiam tales coniunctiones earum ad invicem, etiam si mundus et motus primus esset aeternus. Et propter hoc idem quod modo dictum est, nec secunda pars scientiae astrorum ostendere potest mundum et motum primum esse novum, quia ex quo eosdem quos modo habent, possent habere motus stellae et coniunctiones et virtutes, etiam si mundus et motus primus esset aeternus, tunc

etiam consimiles effectus facere possent in mundo inferiori eis quos modo faciunt, etiam si mundus et motus primus esset aeternus, ergo nec secunda pars scientiae astrorum potest ostendere motum primum et mundum esse novum.

Sicut nec pars prima, nec etiam pars [secunda] mathematicarum scientiarum quae geometria est, potest hoc ostendere. Hoc enim non sequitur ex principiis geometriae, quia oppositum consequentis potest stare cum antecedente, scilicet primum motum et mundum esse aeternum potest stare cum principiis geometriae et omnibus suis conclusionibus. Dato enim hoc falso quod motus primus et mundus sit aeternus, numquid propter hoc erunt principia geometriae falsa, ut "a puncto ad punctum rectam lineam ducere", vel etiam "punctus est, cuius pars non est", et caetera talia, vel etiam suae conclusiones? Constat quod non. Numquid omnes passiones [possibiles] in magnitudine eodem modo essent demonstrabiles de suis substantiis et per easdem causas, etiam si mundus esset aeternus, sicut et si mundus esset novus? Constat quod sic.

Et hoc idem dico de tertia et quarta parte scientiarum mathematicarum quae sunt arithmetica et musica, et per eundem modum ut declaratum est de geometria. Et hoc manifestum est illi qui provectus est in his scientiis et qui scit posse earum.

9. Quod autem nec metaphysicus possit ostendere mundum esse novum, patet sic: mundus dependet ex voluntate divina, sicut ex sua causa sufficiente; sed metaphysicus non potest demonstrare aliquem effectum in duratione posse sequi suam causam sufficientem, sive posse postponi suae causae sufficienti; ergo metaphysicus non potest demonstrare quod mundus sit coaeternus voluntati divinae, mundus sit factus nisi divine.

Item, qui non potest demonstrare hanc fuisse formam voluntatis divinae, ut ab aeterno voluerit mundum producere in hora in qua factus est, ille non potest demonstrare mundum esse novum nec coaeternum voluntati divinae, quia volitum est a volente secundum formam voluntatis; sed metaphysicus non potest demonstrare talem fuisse formam voluntatis divinae ab aeterno: dicere enim quod metaphysicus possit hoc demonstrare, non solum figmento, sed etiam, credo, [cuidam] dementiae simile est: unde enim homini ratio, per quam voluntatem divinam perfecte investiget?

10. Et ex his quae dicta sunt componitur syllogismus: nulla est quaestio cuius conclusio potest ostendi per rationem, quam philosophus non debeat disputare et determinare, quantum per rationem est possibile, ut declaratum est; nullus autem philosophus per rationem potest ostendere motum primum et mundum esse novum, quia nec naturalis, nec mathematicus, nec divinus, ut patet ex praedictis, ergo per nullam rationem humanam potuit ostendi motus primus et mundus esse novus, nec etiam potest ostendi quod sit aeternus; quia qui hoc demonstraret, deberet demonstrare formam voluntatis divinae. Et quis eam investigabit? Ideo dicit Aristoteles, in libro Topicorum, quod "aliquid est problema de quo neutro modo opinamur, ut utrum mundus sit aeternus" vel non. Sunt enim multa in fide quae per rationem demonstrari non possunt, ut quod mortuum redit vivum idem in numero, et quod res generabilis redit sine generatione; et qui his non credit haereticus est, qui autem quaerit scire per rationem fatuus est.

Quia ergo effectus et opera sunt ex virtute, et virtus ex substantia, quis audet dicere se perfecte per rationem cognoscere [substantiam divinam et omnes eius virtutem? Ille dicat se perfecte cognoscere] omnes effectus immediatos Dei: quomodo ex ipso sunt, utrum de novo vel ab aeterno, et quomodo per ipsum in esse conservantur, et quomodo in ipso sunt. Nam in ipso et ex ipso et per ipsum fiunt omnia vel sunt. Et quis est qui hoc possit sufficienter investigare? Et, quia multa sunt de talibus quae fides ponit, quae per rationem humanam investigari non possunt, ideo ubi deficit ratio, ibi suppleat fides, quae confiteri debet potentiam divinam esse super cognitionem humanam. Nec propter hoc decredas articulis fidei, quia demonstrari non possunt aliqui eorum, quia si sic procedas, in nulla lege stabis, eo quod nulla est lex cuius omnes articuli possint demonstrari.

Sic ergo apparet manifeste quod nulla est contradictio inter fidem christianam et philosophiam de aeternitate mundi, si praedicta diligenter inspiciantur, sicut etiam manifestabimus, Deo auxiliante in caeteris quaestionibus, in quibus fides christiana et philosophia superficietenus et hominibus minus diligenter considerantibus videbuntur discordare.

Dicimus ergo quod mundus non est aeternus, sed de novo creattus, quamvis hoc per rationes demonstrari non possit, ut superius visum est, sicut quaedam alia etiam quae pertinent ad fidem: si enim demonstrari possent, non esset fides, sed scientia. Unde pro fide non debet adduci ratio sophistica, [sicut per se patet,] nec ratio dialectica, quia ipsa non facit firmum habitum, sed solum opinionem, et firmior debet esse fides quam opinio, nec ratio demonstrativa, quia tunc fides non esset nisi de his quae demonstrari possent.

11. Tunc ad rationes ad utramque partem adductas respondendum est, et primo ad rationes quae nituntur probare contrarium veritati, scilicet mundum esse Deo coaeternum.

<1> Ad primam. Omne incorruptibile habet virtutem ut semper existat, si intelligas per hoc nomen incorruptibile quod, cum sit ens, non potest deficere neque per corruptionem - de qua loquitur Philosophus in fine I Physicorum: "omne quod corrumpitur, abibit in hoc ultimum", id est in materiam, - nec etiam per corruptionem, largius accipiendo nomen, quam unquam accipit ipse Philosophus, quae scilicet corruptio cadere potest in omni ente quod habet aliam causam, quantum de se est. Nam omnis effectus, quamdiu durat, tamdiu conservatur in esse per aliquam suarum causarum, sicut apparet inducenti; quod autem per aliud in esse conservatur, deficere potest quantum de se est. Si utroque istorum modorum intelligitur incorruptibile, tunc vera est propositio maior quae dicit: omne incorruptibile habet virtutem, ut semper existat; et sic non est incorruptibilis [immo] nec aliquod ens habens aliam causam.

Et tu probas: quod est ingenitum, est incorruptibile. Verum est corruptione quae opponitur generationi, quia sicut generatio est ex materia, sic corruptio sibi opposita est in materiam, scilicet in contrarium et non in puram negationem. Si tamen aliquid sit ingenitum, non oportet quod propter hoc ipsum sit incorruptibile corruptione largius sumpta, quae scilicet est non [in materiam nec] in contrarium, sed in puram negationem, sicut potest corrumpi omne ens causatum circumscripta virtute conservantis. Et hanc conservationem vocabant antiqui philosophi auream catenam, qua omne ens in suo ordine a primo ente conservatur, ipsum autem primum ens, sicut ante se non habet causam, sic ante se non habet conservans. Et, quia iam tactum est quod omne ens [quod est] citra primum conservatur in esse virtute primi principii, ideo magis hoc declaretur.

Et primo per dicta auctorum. In Libro de causis scribitur sic: "Omnis intelligentiae fixio et essentia est per bonitatem puram quae est prima causa." Per eius essentiam intelligit eius productionem in esse, et per eius fixionem intelligit eius durationem. Et, si intelligentia durat per virtutem primi principii, tunc multo magis omnia entia alia. Et huic concordat illud quod scribitur in lege: "ex ipso et per ipsum sunt omnia".

Item, Plato dicit loquens in persona primi principii ipsis inteligentiis haec verba: "plus valent ad aeternitatis vestrae custodiam mea voluntas quam vestra natura".

Et idem ostenditur ratione. Ens causatum non habet de se naturam ut existat, quia, si de se naturam haberet ut existeret, alterius causatum non esset, sed quod durat et in esse conservatur virtute propria et non ex alia virtute superiori, hoc de se habet naturam ut existat; ergo nullum ens causatum in esse conservatur per se. Et ideo, sicut omnia entia quae sunt citra primum principium, sunt ex ipso, sic et per ipsum in esse conservantur, et si primum principium virtutem suam entibus auferret, entia penitus non essent. Et hoc est quod scribitur in Libro de Causis: "omnes virtutes dependentes sunt ex una prima virtute quae est virtus virtutum". Et Averroes Super secundum Metaphysicae loquens de hoc primo principio dicit: "quod illa causa magis est digna et in esse et in virtute quam omnia entia; omnia enim entia non acquirunt esse et virtutem nisi ab ista causa; est igitur ipsum ens per se et verum per se, et omnia entia alia [sunt] sunt entia et vera per esse et per veritatem eius".

Item, virtus quae facit durationem aeternam, est virtus infinita, quia, si esset finita, tunc posset accipi virtus maior; ergo, cum non possit esse duratio maior quam sit duratio aeterna, sequeretur quod virtus maior non faceret maiorem durationem quam virtus minor, quod est impossibile; sed in nullo ente causato est virtus infinita, quia omne causatum est per transitum, sive per factionem acceptum, et hoc repugnat virtuti infinitae.

Hoc idem etiam probatur ex alio. Quia virtus primi motoris maior est quam virtus alicuius motoris posterioris et infinito non potest aliquid esse maius, ergo in nullo ente causato est virtus infinita, nec duratio aeterna per se, sed per virtutem primi principii cuius virtus per se est aeterna et infinita. Et declaratur ratio: sicut duratione quae semper est non potest accipi maior duratio, sic oportet quod virtus quae facit durationem quae semper est sive aeterna, sit talis quod ea non potuit accipi virtus maior, et talis solum est virtus infinita.

<2> Ad secundam rationem dicendum. Cum dicis: illud est aeternum quod non habet ante se aliquam durationem, dico quod falsum est. Licet enim tempus non sit ante mundum, aeternitas tamen est ante mundum: ipsa enim semper est. Tu dicis: illud nunquam est quod habet ante se durationem aeternam. Dico quod non oportet. Illud enim novum quod hodie factum est, habet ante se durationem aeternam, quia ipsam aeternitatem quae semper est, et tamen non est dicere quod ipsum nunquam est.

<3> Ad tertiam rationem dicendum quod, licet ens, cuius productio est ex subiecto et materia, sive per generationem, dependeat ex duplici potentia, scilicet ex potentia activa sui agentis et ex potentia suae materiae, nihil enim fit ex materia, nisi illud ad quod ipsa habuit potentiam passivam, tamen illa quorum factio non est generatio nec ex materia, illa solum dependent ex sola potentia agentis principii, non materiae. Quomodo enim potes dicere quod illud dependet ex potentia materiae cuius productio non est ex materia, sicut est mundus? Apparet enim cuilibet quod factio mundi non potuit esse generatio. Unde, si non esset alius modus fiendi nisi generatio, nihil universaliter esset factum. Dico ergo quod mundus factus est et de novo factus est, quia non est coaeternus Deo. Et cum dicis: ergo potuit fieri, dico quod verum est: potuit fieri sola potentia agentis, non subiecti et materiae. Et quia iam in solutione tactum est quod aliquis effectus sufficienter dependeat ex sola potentia agentis, de quo aliquis dubitaret, ideo hoc declaratur sic:

Omne illud cuius factio dependet ex materia, si materia non sit, ipsum [esse] impossibile est; totum ens quod est citra primum principium, factum est, quia causam habet, et illud voco ens factum quod habet aliam suae productionis; si ergo omnis factio dependet a materia, et nulla ex sola potentia agentis principii, et praeter totum ens quod est citra primum principium non erat materia aliqua, sequitur quod totum ens, quod est primum principium, esset impossibile; factum est ergo aliquid quod est impossibile esset fieri.

<4> Ad quartam rationem dicendum. Cum dicis: omne novum factum est per transmutationem, verum est solum de entibus quorum factio est per generationem: nam solum in generabilibus invenitur transmutatio. Unde et corpora caelestia quae habent substantias ingenitas, sicut transmutantur secundum situm, sic et generantur secundum situm.

<5> Ad quintam rationem. Cum dicis: omne novum est in tempore, quoniam novum in aliqua duratione debet fieri in aliqua parte eius, quoniam si esset simul cum qualibet parte durationis illius, non esset novum in illa duratione, et sola duratio quae partes habet, tempus est, dico ad hoc quod aliquid potest dici novum duobus modis: aut quia est, cum prius non esset, sed habendo esse post suum contradictorium, non quod sit in aliqua parte durationis in qua est, et in alia non; et sic mundus est novus, et tale novum non oportet esse in tempore. Alio modo potest aliquid dici novum, quia in aliqua parte durationis in qua est, habet esse, in alia parte non-esse; et omne quod sic novum est, necessario est in tempore, quia sola duratio quae partes habet, tempus est; et sic mundus non est novus. Unde mundus in nulla duratione potest esse novus: non in tempore, quia mundus incepit cum tempore, ideo nulla pars temporis antecedit mundum; nec in aeternitate, quia aeternitas est indivisibilis, et quod est in aeternitate, semper uno modo se habet.

<6> Ad sextam rationem dicendum. Cum dicis: omnis generatio est ex corrupto, verum est. Cum dicis secundo: omne corruptum prius est generatum, dico quod istam propositionem concedit naturalis, quia ipse ex suis principiis non potest ponere factionem rei generabilis et corruptibilis nisi per generationem. Qui tamen ponit factionem rei generabilis non esse per generationem, sicut debet ponere qui ponit primum hominem - homo enim est

res generabilis, et eius productio non potest esse per generationem, si sit primus - ipse debet negare illam propositionem quae dicit: omne corruptum prius est generatum, quia ipsa contradicit suae positioni; primus enim homo aliquando corruptus est, cum tamen nunquam fuerit generatus. Unde illa ratio sexta innititur principiis naturalibus, et dictum est superius quod qui ponit mundum esse factum novum, dimittere debet causas naturales et quaerere causam superiorem.

<7> Ad septimam rationem dicendum. Cum dicis quod effectus in duratione non potest sequi suam causam sufficientem, dicendum quod hoc verum est de causa agente per naturam, non de agente voluntarie. Sicut enim Deus aeterno intellectu potest nova intelligere, licet illa respectu sui non sint nova, sic aeterna voluntate potest nova agere.

<8> Ad octavam rationem dicendum. Quod potens et volens de necessitate agit, hoc est verum in hora ad quam voluntas est determinata. Modo, licet aeterna sit potestas Dei qua potuit mundum facere, et voluntas qua voluit, quia tamen illa voluntas solum erat respectu horae in qua mundus factus sit, ideo mundus est novus, licet voluntas Dei sit aeterna.

<9> Ad aliam rationem dicendum. Cum dicis: omnis effectus novus aliquam requirit novitatem in aliquo suorum principiorum, dico quod illud non oportet in agente per voluntatem, quia secundum antiquam voluntatem possunt fieri actiones novae praeter hoc quod facta sit transmutatio in voluntate vel in volente. Ad confirmationem rationis dicendum quod non solum potuit agens agere novum effectum, quia ipsum habet novam substantiam, aut, quia ipsum habet aliquam novam virtutem vel situm, vel, quia prius subiacebat impedimento, aut, quia in suo passivo ex quo agit, facta est nova dispositio, sed etiam aliquod agens potest producere effectum novum per hoc quod ipsum habet voluntatem aeternam determinatam ad aliquam horam in qua vult agere, secundum illam voluntatem.

<10> Ad sequentem rationem dicendum est quod non oportet quod omne quod movetur post quietem reducatur ad motum aeternum, sed oportet quod

omne quod movetur post quietem reducatur ad motum primum sicut ad aliquam suam causam qui non est post quietem; unde licet motus primus sit novus, ipse tamen non est post quietem: non enim quaelibet immobilitas quies est, sed immobilitas eius quod natum est moveri, ut scribitur III Physicorum. Et ante motum primum non erat aliquod mobile natum moveri, et dico ante in duratione.

<11> Ad aliam rationem dicendum. Cum dicis: voluntas quae postponit volitum, exspectat aliquid in futuro, verum est solum de voluntate cuius actio est in tempore, quia solum in tempore est futuratio et exspectatio, sed de voluntate cuius actio est ante tempus, non est hoc verum; et actio voluntatis divinae est ante tempus, saltem illa qua mundum et tempus agebat.

<12> Ad sequentem rationem dicendum est quod illa duo quae sunt in eadem duratione, simul sunt, si nulla pars durationis illius cadit inter illa, sicut duo temporalia simul sunt in tempore inter quae nulla pars temporis cadit; si tamen inter aliqua duo nulla cadit duratio propter hoc quod unum est in nunc aeternitatis et alterum est in nunc temporis, et sic nulla inter ea cadit duratio, non oportet quod talia sint simul. Sic se habet voluntas Dei quae est in nunc aeternitatis, et factio mundi quae est in nunc temporis.

<13> Ad aliam rationem dicendum, sicut dicebatur. Tu arguis in contrarium, quia ponere talem formam voluntatis in Deo, hoc est fingere. Dicendum quod non est verum: non enim omnia figmenta sunt quae demonstrari non possunt.

Ad illud quod tu secundo arguis, dico quod ex quo fuerit talis forma voluntatis divinae ab aeterno, talem oportuit esse modum procedendi voliti ex voluntate, ut volitum perfecte sit sic conforme voluntati.

<14> Ad sequentem rationem dicendum. Cum dicis: ab antiqua voluntate inter quam et suum effectum non cadit transmutatio, non potest fieri novus effectus, hoc solum verum est de voluntate a qua procedit effectus per transmutationem; talis non est voluntas divina.

<15> Ad aliud dico quod illud exemplum in aliquo est conveniens, licet non perfecte.

Rationes ad partem oppositam gratia conclusionis concedantur, licet solvi possint, cum sint sophisticae.

12. Ex his ergo apparet quod philosophum dicere aliquid esse possibile vel impossibile, hoc est illud: dicere esse possibile vel impossibile per rationes investigabiles ab homine. Statim enim quando aliquis dimittit rationes, cessat esset philosophus, nec innititur philosophia revelationibus et in miraculis. Cum ergo tu ipse dicis et dicere debes multa esse vera, quae tamen, si non affirmes vera nisi quantum ratio humana te inducere potest, illa nunquam concedere debes, sicut est ressurectio hominum quam ponit fides. Et bene enim in talibus creditur auctoritati divinae et non rationi humanae. Quaeram enim a te: quae ratio hoc demonstrat? Quaeram etiam: quae ratio demonstrat rem generabilem post suam corruptionem iterum redire sine generatione, et etiam eandem in numero quae prius ante suam corruptionem erat, sicut oportet fieri in resurrectione hominum secundum sententiam nostrae fidei? Philosophus tamen in fine II De generatione dicit rem corruptam posse redire eandem in specie, sed non eandem in numero. Nec propter hoc contradicit fidei, quia ipse dicit hoc non esse possibile secundum causas naturales. Ex talibus enim ratiocinatur naturalis. Fides autem nostra dicit hoc esse possibile per causam superiorem quae est principium et finis nostrae fidei, Deus gloriosus et benedictus.

13. Ideo non est contradictio inter fidem et philosophum. Quare ergo murmuras contra philosophum, cum idem secum concedis? Nec credas quod philosophus qui vitam suam posuit in studio sapientiae, contradixit veritati fidei catholicae in aliquo, sed magis studeas, quia modicum habes intellectum respectu philosophorum qui fuerunt et sunt sapientes mundi, ut possis intelligere sermones eorum. Sermo enim magistri intelligendus est ad melius, nec valet quod dicunt quidam maligni ponentes studium suum ad hoc quod possint invenire rationes repugnantes in aliquo veritati christianae fidei, quod tamen procul dubio est impossibile. Dicunt enim quod christianus, secundum quod huiusmodi, non potest esse philosophus, quia ex lege sua cogitur

destruere principia philosophiae. Illud enim falsum est, quia christianus concedit conclusionem per rationes philosophicas conclusam non posse aliter se habere per illa per quae concluditur, et si concludatur per causas naturales. Quod mortuum non redibit vivum immediate idem numero, hoc concedit non posse aliter se habere per causas naturales per quas concluditur; concedit tamen hoc posse se aliter habere per causam superiorem quae est causa totius naturae et totius entis causati. Ideo christianus subtiliter intelligens non cogitur ex lege sua destruere principia philosophiae, sed salvat fidem et philosophiam, neutram corripiendo. Si autem aliquis in dignitate constitutus sive non, et tam ardua non possit intelligere, tunc oboediat sapientiori et credat legi christianae, non propter rationem sophisticam, quia ipsa fallit, nec propter rationem dialecticam, quia ipsa non facit ita firmum habitum, sicut est fides, quia conclusio rationis dialecticae accipitur cum formidine alterius partis, nec per rationem demonstrativam, tum quia non est possibilis in omnibus quae ponit lex nostra, tum quia ipsa facit scientiam. "Est enim demonstratio syllogismus faciens scire", ut scribitur I Posteriorum, et fides non est scientia. Hinc legi Christi quemlibet christianum adhaerere et credere secundum quod oportet faciat auctor eiusdem legis Christus gloriosus qui est Deus benedictus in saecula saeculorum. Amen.

The Scriptorium Project is the work of a small group of lay people of various apostolic churches who are interested in the preservation, transmission, and translation of the works of the early and medieval church. Our efforts are to make the works of the church fathers accessible to anyone who might have an interest in Christian antiquities and the theological, philosophical, and moral writings that have become the bedrock of Western Civilization.

To-date, our releases have pulled from the Greek, Syriac, Georgian, Latin, Nordic, Slavic, Arabic, Frankish, Celtic, Ethiopian, and Coptic traditions of Christianity, and have been pulled from sundry local traditions and languages.

Other Titles from the Nordic Church (Norway, Sweden, Denmark):

Of the Highest Good by Boethius of Dacia (Dec. 2007)
Privileges & Oaths by Magnus VI, King of Norway (Apr. 2008)
Non Parum Animus Noster by Pope Alexander III (May 2008)
Revelations- Book I by St. Bridget of Sweden (June 2008)
The Eternity of the World by Boethius of Dacia (Aug. 2008)
Letter on the Institutes of the Law by Magnus VI, King of Norway (Nov. 2023)
Letters from the North: Catholic Missionaries in Scandinavia (Dec. 2023)

www.ingramcontent.com/pod-product-compliance
Lightning Source LLC
LaVergne TN
LVHW061603070526
838199LV00077B/7153